MOTORCYCLES
A GUIDE TO THE WORLD'S BEST BIKES™

SUZUKI
BUILT FOR SPEED

rosen publishing's
rosen central

NEW YORK

Published in 2014 by The Rosen Publishing Group, Inc.
29 East 21st Street, New York, NY 10010

First Edition

Library of Congress Cataloging-in-Publication Data

Bailey, Diane, 1966–
Suzuki: built for speed/Diane Bailey.—First edition.
    pages cm.—(Motorcycles: a guide to the world's best bikes)
Includes bibliographical references and index.
ISBN 978-1-4777-1858-2 (library binding)—ISBN 978-1-4777-1876-6 (pbk.)—
ISBN 978-1-4777-1877-3 (6-pack)
1. Suzuki motorcycle. I. Title.
TL448.S8B35 2013
629.227'5—dc23

2013023152

Manufactured in the United States of America

CPSIA Compliance Information: Batch #W14YA: For further information, contact Rosen Publishing, New York, New York, at 1-800-237-9932.

CONTENTS

INTRODUCTION

michio Suzuki wasn't thinking about motorcycles. At least he wasn't in 1909, when he founded the Suzuki company. Instead, the Japanese businessman started his company to sell looms for weaving, which was big business in Japan. By the 1950s, the Japanese needed affordable transportation, so in 1951, Suzuki built a motor that could be attached to a bicycle. The "Power Free" had an engine displacement of just 36 cc (2.2 cubic inches), with only one horsepower. It didn't go far or fast on the road, but it had the power necessary to launch Suzuki as a force in the Japanese motorcycle market. Suzuki soon upgraded the "cyclemotor," and the company officially changed its name to Suzuki Motor Company. Soon, it branched out into manufacturing actual motorcycles. Over the next two decades, it became a major brand in the Japanese market.

The Suzuki racing team, nicknamed "Team Yellow" because of the company colors, has brought home awards in all segments of motorcycle racing, with bikes like the RM-Z450 eating up the track at supercross events, and its supersport GSX-R machines dominating in superbike racing.

Today, Suzuki is probably best known for its supersport line of motorcycles, including the legendary Hayabusa, which set a record for the fastest bike on the market. It was almost singly responsible for starting the hypersport craze in the late 1990s. Added to that are the line of GSX-R "Gixxer" racers, which debuted in the 1980s with the GSX-750R, a bike that redefined the class. But Suzuki recognized that not all riders are racers, and so it worked to satisfy a slightly more mellow market with "semisport" bikes like the SV650. Rounding out its product line is a broad range of cruisers, tourers, and standard bikes. All of them are underscored by the engineering for which Suzuki is respected. Their bikes combine superior reliability with innovative design. They are indeed "built for speed."

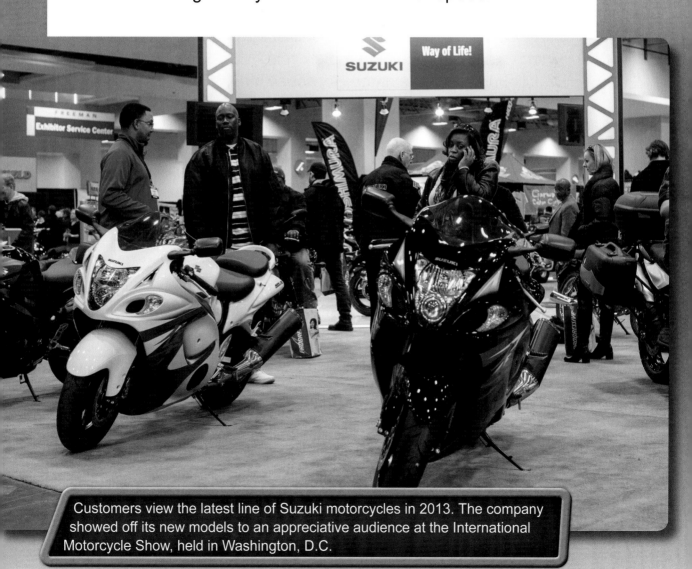

Customers view the latest line of Suzuki motorcycles in 2013. The company showed off its new models to an appreciative audience at the International Motorcycle Show, held in Washington, D.C.

CHAPTER ONE

THE HAYABUSA

Ask a Hayabusa rider what the biggest downside to this motorcycle is, and the answer might be, "the chance of getting a speeding ticket." Suzuki introduced the Hayabusa in 1999, ending the century with what instantly became a motorcycle classic. Indeed, with a top speed of 188 mph (302 kph), the 'Busa was dubbed the "world's fastest production motorcycle."

In Japanese, the name *Hayabusa* means "peregrine falcon," a name Suzuki chose to reflect the bike's amazing speed. In the air, the peregrine falcon is the fastest bird in the world. It can fly about 200 mph (322 kph) as it swoops in for its prey. And just what is that prey? The falcon prefers blackbirds. That also happened to be the nickname of a competing motorcycle from Honda, the CBR1100XX. When Suzuki unveiled the Hayabusa, the message was clear: blackbird, watch out.

The Hayabusa GSX1300R impressed the motorcycle world when it came out, and Suzuki hasn't messed with success too much in the years that have followed. Nearly fifteen years later, the bike is still a dominant player in the hypersport market. With its stacked headlight and LED taillight, sleek full fairing, and bold color options, the Hayabusa turns heads. According to Ultimate Motorcycling, "The rebellious styling and powerful look can stop people in the street and attract envious stares."

The Hayabusa is built to put the road in the rear-view mirror at smoking speeds. Fuel injection immediately breathes life into the four-cylinder, liquid-cooled engine, which roars up to a 11,000 rpm redline. Its 1,340 cc (82 cubic inches) displacement engine is definitely a "Big Gulp," making it Suzuki's largest sport bike. There's enough room to comfortably give the bike 179 horsepower at 9,600 rpm, and 107 lb-ft of torque. Where the Hayabusa excels—or maybe it should be accels, as in "accelerates"—is in a straight line. With no bumps, no curves, and no distractions, the 'Busa rips down the road like no other. It can cover a quarter mile in

With its white body and blue accents, the Hayabusa proves that it's Suzuki's signature motorcycle. Here, it claims the floor at the Thailand International Motor Expo in Bangkok in 2011.

9.81 seconds at 145.6 mph (234.3 kph), with a zero-to-sixty time of just over 2.5 seconds.

Just because the Hayabusa is designed for open-road and three-digit speed limit signs doesn't mean it doesn't offer some versatility. It comes with a choice of three drive modes on the engine. Those can be adjusted depending on driving conditions and the driver's preferences. One engine map is ideal for cruising on freeways, for example, while another is designed to better take on the challenges of a twisting mountain road.

A NEW STANDARD FOR SPEED

The race was on. When the Hayabusa came out, it set a new speed record. With a top speed of 188 mph (302 kph), it beat Honda's CBR1100XX by a staggering 10 mph (16 kph). Soon, word on the street was that Kawasaki was going to raise the stakes even more when it released the Ninja ZX-12R in 2000. That bike, it was said, was going to hit the 200 mph (322 kph) mark. Higher speeds mean a higher risk for deadly accidents, however. That made politicians in Europe nervous. They hinted that they might ban imports of motorcycles that were simply too fast. At that point the Japanese manufacturers backed off, reaching an informal agreement not to produce bikes that were any faster than 186 mph (300 kph). The agreement only applied to street-legal production bikes, which are available to be sold to the public. Bikes designed exclusively for racing can still go faster.

Part Bruiser, Part Cruiser

The heavyweight Hayabusa is big and bold, weighing in at a hefty 573 pounds (260 kg). To handle the bulk, the Hayabusa uses a twin-spar chassis design, made of lightweight but strong aluminum, and sits on a 58.3-inch (1,480 mm) wheelbase. An aluminum alloy swingarm adds to the Hayabusa's sleek, distinctive styling that is easily recognizable among enthusiasts. It looks good, but it's not just for show: those lines are carefully crafted to make the Hayabusa a top performer in aerodynamics. The company tests both bike and rider in a wind tunnel to find the best angles to reduce friction from the wind—and save gas as well.

The suspension takes a page from Goldilocks—not too firm, not too soft. An inverted front fork and single rear shock are both fully adjustable for preload and compression and rebound damping. The bike is comfortable enough for a longer ride, but it never loses the feeling of being on a power machine, not the living room couch. Around corners, it offers good flickability—side-to-side responsiveness—combined with solid stability. Brembo Monobloc calipers on twin discs in the front, and a single disc in the rear, provide braking power. The pistons were enlarged for 2013 to give better braking control, and Suzuki also added an antilock braking system (ABS) for additional performance.

The 'Busa hit the market as the fastest bike out there. Now that it's getting on in years, it's got some competition from newer models from other manufacturers, such as Kawasaki's

Painted in a candy red that begs to be noticed, the aggressive styling of the Hayabusa has grabbed the attention of motorcycle riders and enthusiasts around the globe. It's on display here in Istanbul, Turkey.

Ninja ZX-14R or BMW's S1000RR. For all-around performance, though, and comfort that can take a rider more than a few miles, the Hayabusa has clearly earned its status as the granddaddy of the supersports. Visor Down sums it up: "Despite [other bikes] being technologically more advanced and easier to live with day to day, the Hayabusa remains the cult bike in this class and one you owe it to yourself to ride."

CHAPTER TWO

LITER OF THE PACK

Sometimes, it's not about the specs. Sure, the GSX-R1000 has some impressive numbers, but what gives this sport bike its special something isn't listed in the statistics. Instead, it's that hard-to-define quality. Call it personality, charisma, or soul. Call it attitude. In flat-out tests, there are other bikes that are faster or lighter. There are other bikes that handle a little more smoothly or are a little better looking. But there's something about the "Gixxer" that shines. According to *Motorcycle USA*, "Visit any motorcycle road race and you'll notice Suzuki's GSX-R1000 sportbike is the most prevalent machine on the grid. The Suzuki literbike has carved a niche based on its immediate out-of-the-crate performance, not to mention how straightforward it is to convert into a full-on racer."

At the heart of the GSX-R1000 is a liquid-cooled, inline four-cylinder engine, with a full liter (999 cc, 61 cubic inches) displacement that gives this bike its power. Unlike some superbikes, this one doesn't start to show off only at the higher revs. Instead, the powerband stays consistent throughout the range, and it delivers smoothly throughout the middle and higher numbers. Recent models boast improved throttle sensitivity, and the tall first gear lets the Gixxer climb to 100 mph (161 kph) without shifting. That makes it convenient on a commute or other ordinary riding where triple-digit speeds are not required—or legal.

True, some riders like the dragon breath–fueled acceleration at the higher ranges, but this bike offers solid performance that is predictable without being boring. And face it: it's hard to get bored when the GSX-R1000 zips through a a 0-to-60 run in 2.9 seconds or digests a quarter mile of track in just over 10 seconds at 144 mph (232 kph). The Gixxer reaches maximum torque with 79.2 lb-ft at 10,400 revs, and boasts 168 horsepower at 11,800 rpm before redlining at 13,300 rpm. Lower the face mask, and bugs beware.

Suzuki celebrated the 70th International Motorcycle Exhibition, held in Milan, Italy, with its own version of a classic: the GSXR-1000. The company's literbike remains a performance leader in its class.

The Gixxer is a race bike, but it's also well suited for everyday use because of its friendly handling. At the curb, it weighs in at 448 pounds (203 kg), with a wheelbase of 55.3 inches (1,405 mm). The overall size, proportions, and ergonomics work for a variety of rider sizes (although very small riders may feel it's a bit overwhelming).

A MILLION STRONG

The GSX line began three decades ago, in 1984, when Suzuki manufactured the GSX-400. However, that bike was only available in Japan. U.S. customers would have to hold on another year, until 1985, to get a Gixxer. It was worth the wait. The bigger and better GSX-R750 was considered one of the first modern race replica bikes—meaning it very closely resembled models used in racing conditions. In an era before superbikes had hit 1,000 cc (61 cubic inches), the 750 was an immediate hit. Suzuki introduced the GSX-1100 in 1986 as a larger version, but then downsized in 2001 to an even thousand with the GSX-R1000. A baby brother, the "Gixxer Sixxer" with 600 cc (37 cubic inches), is also available.

In 2012, Suzuki produced the one millionth GSX-R bike. The company commemorated the event with a special limited edition of the GSX-R1000, which has developed a cult following and remains the company's signature sport bike. That's not exactly a surprise, considering it's been ridden by numerous AMA Superbike champions, won World Superbike and World Endurance championships, and has racked up numerous other titles in the last decade.

The Perfect Date

The GSX-R1000 faces a lot of stiff competition in the superbike category, with other bikes offering some extras that the Gixxer doesn't. The Honda CBR1000RR has an ABS (antilock brake system) option, while Yamaha's YZF-R1 and Kawasaki's Ninja ZX-10R both offer traction control. However, most test riders reported that the lack of traction control was a bigger drawback

Get those knees up: taking corners at a forty-five-degree angle, the Gixxer offers a powerful but smooth ride. French rider Matthieu Gines chooses the GSX-R1000 for a motorcycle endurance race in 2010.

on paper than it was in practice because the Suzuki's handling communicates potential problems to the rider with enough time to correct them. Also, three drive-mode selectors—easily changeable at the press of a button—allow riders to adjust the power input and address traction problems.

Some riders object to the bike's being slightly less powerful overall in comparison to others in its class. However, others find it more manageable. That easier handling can help riders feel more comfortable and confident. Even if European bikes from Ducati and Aprilia are a little faster, most riders won't actually ride them fast enough that it's important to shave off another tenth of a second in a race.

Beyond that, the GSX-R1000 has a certain recognizable style about it, with its distinctive blue-and-white color scheme, trapezoid-shaped headlight, and red pinstriping outlining the wheels. Adjustable footpegs accommodate different-sized riders, and the saddle material gives added grip, for less sliding when coming out of a fast turn. In 2012, Suzuki also improved the torque delivery, lightened the pistons by 11 percent, and replaced the dual exhaust pipes with a single vent that also reduced the bike's overall weight. Ventilation holes in the engine were upgraded to a pentagonal shape that lets the engine suck air and accelerate faster. Monoblock Brembo caliper brakes offer superb stopping power.

The Gixxer is versatile. That's not always the word that seems most desirable when describing a race bike, but Suzuki should not be underestimated. It has created a bike that

The name says it all: Italian company Brembo is known for its high-performance brakes for cars and motorcycles. On the Gixxer, its monoblock caliper brakes keep the bike in line.

oozes power, while still being comfortable and reliable. The Gixxer proves that the perfect date isn't always the one with the thousand-watt smile. It's the one you want to hang out with all night.

CHAPTER THREE

ON THE BOULEVARD

In the movies, the typical Japanese motorcycle—usually topped with black-masked bad guys—is a sleek and sporty affair, designed to take corners at blistering speeds and elude any pursuers. But with the Boulevard M109R, Suzuki has added some weight—764 pounds (347 kg), to be exact—to its lineup. This full-size cruiser offers the comfort of a big tourer but throws in some of Suzuki's signature speediness to rev things up.

Even the name of the M109R speaks to its power. That "M" can be said to represent the muscle in the machine, and the 109 takes inventory of the cubic inch volume of the engine. Pull out the metric converter and put that number into ccs, and that's 1,783 of them in the engine. That's plenty and more to power this bad boy down the road. It's expected that a power cruiser will perform in straight-line acceleration, but the M109R ups the ante in this class. The massive displacement of the engine is joined by technology borrowed from Suzuki's GSX line of sport bikes. That gives it a little extra zing not often found in a bike this size.

Suzuki's most powerful cruiser comes with a sturdy, double-cradle steel-tube chassis that can support this bike's weight, and reversed front forks offer even more strength and stability. Its low center of gravity makes it surprisingly easy to handle for its size. Rubber mounts absorb the vibration, so

A look at the control panel on Suzuki's Boulevard M109R gives riders a color-coded and easily readable guide to revs, speed, and other specs about the Boulevard's performance.

a long ride won't result in a layer of enamel chattered off the rider's teeth. At 67.3 inches (1,710 mm), the long wheelbase offers a good combination of stability and maneuverability. Meanwhile, the rear tire measures 240 mm (9.4 inches) wide, making it the biggest Suzuki has ever used on a motorcycle. It sacrifices a little in the cornering category, but gives the M109R a smoother ride.

Part of the cruiser culture is looks, and the M109R doesn't disappoint. Chrome accents brighten the overall appearance,

WHO'S THE BOSS?

Suzuki needed to find some middle ground in its cruiser line, which jumped from 800 cc (49 cubic inches) engines to 1,800 cc (110 cubic inches). The company filled the gap with the Boulevard C90T B.O.S.S. (Blacked Out Special Suzuki), a newly introduced model designed in a classic cruiser style. "Classic," in this case, means the design is neither out-there extreme nor ho-hum boring. The all-black matte finish is broken up with just a few well-placed chrome accents used on the cylinder heads, turn signals, and headlight cover.

Suzuki borrowed the shape of the steel-tube chassis and swingarm from the M90 platform, and then outfitted the B.O.S.S. with a 1,462 cc (89 cubic inches), V-twin motor, and a smooth five-gear tranny. Together, they let the bike pull easily through the gears and revs. At 800 pounds (363 kg), it's not exactly a lightweight, but the weight handles well once the bike gets rolling. Comfort rules on the the B.O.S.S., which comes with generous wiggle room, a comfortably low seating position (but not so low as to risk knee-scraping), and cushy suspension for long trips. A carefully designed windscreen minimizes wind buffeting and integrated saddlebags provide ample packing room.

while giving it just enough of a retro feel to seem like an authentic touring bike. It's not just looks, though. *Ultimate Motorcycling* reports, "Instinctively, even non-motorcyclists sense that this motorcycle is not merely attractive; it radiates an abundance of performance clout."

A Polite Monster

Crack open the engine to find a digital fuel-injected, liquid-cooled V-twin engine. It thrives on a dual throttle valve that makes the engine purr even when the revs are low and gives it enough oomph to get off the line fast. Suzuki is known for its electronic fuel injection system, which automatically regulates air intake and speed. The M109R grumbles nicely on the low end, but

A rider keeps Suzuki's Boulevard M109R in its element, cruising down a boulevard with plenty of power. Suzuki's gleaming machine joins cruiser comfort with extra performance borrowed from its sportbikes.

rev up over 4,000 rpm and the Boulevard really hits its stride. Pushing all that power are massive, 112 mm (4.4 inches) pistons that are the largest in any motorcycle, or even car, in mass production today. But their size doesn't slow them down. They are made of a forged aluminum alloy that keeps them lightweight and resistant to internal friction.

All of this adds up to great numbers. The M109R boasts 127 ponies at 6,200 rpm, and 117 lb-ft of torque at 3,200 revs. The zero-to-sixty run takes just under four seconds, and a skilled rider can coax out a quarter mile in about eleven seconds—not a race time, but not exactly slouchy on a cruiser. In fact, the five-gear transmission sometimes feels a bit limiting for an engine growling to be let loose up to its 7,500 redline. According to Motorcycle.com, "A quick twist of the wrist can send your eyeballs bouncing to the back of your head and the bike rearing up on its haunches like a spooked racehorse. Just how we like it....Fortunately, Suzuki has [created] a monster machine with polite manners."

There's also plenty of electronic wizardry. Suzuki loaded the M109R with sophisticated electronics that keep the bike fine-tuned to a host of riding conditions. For example, each cylinder comes with a pair of spark plugs that are controlled individually. They fire together during an easy ride, but split up and perform a relay when the gas is really flowing, which lowers the emissions.

When it's time to slow things down, the brakes are worthy of a racer, with four-piston calipers on twin discs in front and dual-piston calipers on the rear single. The Suzuki outperformed its rivals on the zero-to-one hundred-to-zero speed test, completing the turnaround in just under fifteen seconds.

Of course, a touring bike is about comfort, and the M109R satisfies in that category, too. Forward footing makes for a relaxed posture, especially for taller riders. Fortunately, comfortable ergonomics for long-term riding don't come at the expense of control: Its pilots aren't being taken for a ride; they're definitely directing the action. Overall, the M109R is the ultimate muscle cruiser—a blend of comfort and raw power, all with an attitude.

CHAPTER FOUR

TAKE IT OUTSIDE

When a company wants feedback on its products, it often asks its customers what they think. That's exactly what Suzuki did when it was updating the RM-Z450. In fact, Suzuki went straight to its VIP customers: the company racers for Team Yellow. After all, who would know better than a professional racer, skilled at riding Suzukis, what would make this off-roading dirt bike even better? Suzuki tapped into the knowledge of motocross riders like Brett Metcalfe, Ricky Carmichael, and James Stewart to fine-tune the already impressive RM-Z450.

Suzuki didn't want to mess with success too much. After all, it was the Z450 that rookie rider Ryan Dungey rode to the top of the podium in 2010, for both the AMA motocross and supercross competitions. Instead, Suzuki has let the Z450 continue to prove itself as a reliable workhorse, while still tweaking it to improve performance.

At the core of the Z450 is a 449 cc (27 cubic inches), four-stroke, single cylinder, liquid-cooled DOHC engine. A five-speed transmission gives the rider a little extra flexibility depending on terrain, and shifting stays smooth from first gear on up the ladder. Although early models of the Z450 gave easy access to power at the bottom, they tended to top out too early. An improved engine in later models fixed that, offering a solid

Supercross and motocross star James Stewart takes a jump at the AMA Monster Energy Supercross in 2013 in Atlanta, Georgia. The factory racing version of the RM-Z450 conforms well to Stewart's individual style.

pull into the upper ranges. The RM-Z450 produces 51.9 horse-power at 8,900 revs, and delivers 33.2 lb-ft of torque at 7,600 rpm. That's solid mid-range power before the engine redlines at about 11,000 rpm.

One thing Suzuki knows how to do well is feed its engines. The company dominates in fuel-injection technology, and the Z450 benefits from years of testing and tinkering. When the bike topped the podium in motocross and Supercross championships, it was the first motocross bike to do so using a fuel-injection system. Suzuki uses a sophisticated electronic system that responds to changes in airflow so that the throttle runs smoothly throughout the rpm range,

SOUP IT UP

The RM-Z450 is a great bike straight off the showroom floor, but professional motocrossers and supercrossers like to tinker with things anyway. In 2012, racer James Stewart joined the Suzuki team. Shortly after, test rider Rich Taylor got a chance to ride Stewart's personalized Z450. Taylor tested Suzuki bikes for many years and has ridden several racers' bikes. He said of Stewart's bike, "His setup is a lot different than the normal race team setup." For one thing, "He runs the gnarliest, stiffest forks I've almost ever tested." That suits Stewart's riding style, which is far out front, transferring his weight over the front wheel. Taylor also reported that the power on the bike was a little broader than that of a production version of the machine, and very smooth. "The slowest amateur guy would get on this bike and he could handle it."

with a twelve-hole fuel/air mister that delivers precisely the right blend. The Z450 also comes with two coupler plugs that can be attached to modify the fuel supply. One lightens things up to keep a snappy throttle response; the other richens the fuel to soften the overall power blast.

Inside the power plant, engineers switched to a lighter piston that revs fast and breathes life into the bike quickly at the lower end, and delivers torque through the middle. The piston pin is shorter and covered in a special coating that reduces friction.

A close-up of the RM-Z450 shows the Separate Function Fork (SFF) on the front suspension, which has adjustable compression and rebound damping, better stability, and reduces the bike's weight.

Take Turns

"No one will contradict this statement: the Suzuki RM-Z450 is the best-turning 450cc motocross bike ever made." So said *Motocross Action* magazine, adding, "It makes swift direction changes, as though the front end were attached to a roller-coaster track. It is thrilling to dive inside of every bike on the track—and know that the other riders can't do anything to stop you (unless they are on Suzukis also)."

In the twisties, testers noted the bike handled more like a lightweight and manageable two-stroke instead of a four-stroke. The 58.9-inch (1,496 mm) wheelbase carries the bike's 244 pounds (111 kg) neatly through turns.

For 2013, the Z450 got a Separate Function Fork (SFF) for the front suspension, which has adjustable compression and rebound damping. The split system shaved 2 percent off the overall weight of the bike, and the slightly extended diameter at the front fork gives it a bit more stability. The rear shock has adjustable spring preload, compression, and rebound damping.

Change one thing and you have to change another, so Suzuki also turned its attention to the twin-spar aluminum chassis and swingarm to produce a slender frame offering both strength and balance. Braking is handled by double-piston calipers on the front disc and a single piston on the rear. The seat is designed with a special grip pattern to keep riders safely in the saddle.

Suzuki is happy to boast about most of the changes on the updated bike, but it's keeping quiet on one thing: engineers

Although an injury later sidelined him, Supercross and motocross rider James Stewart rode Suzuki's RM-Z450 in a stellar 2013 performance at the AMA Monster Energy Supercross event in Atlanta, Georgia.

shushed the Z450 with a new silencer. It keeps the bike's overall noise output low enough to meet the ninety-four-decibel limit imposed by the American Motorcyclist Association (AMA) without sacrificing power output.

Handling can be tricky to master for novices, but with a little practice, the Z450 delivers, acting like the racehorse it is. It might need a little coaxing, but once you bond with the animal, it's yours, and *Cycle World* awarded the bike its "Best Motocrosser" title in 2012. The RM-Z450 does face stiff competition from others in its class, such as the CRF450R from Honda, the 450SX-F from KTM, or Yamaha's YZ450F. How to choose? In this case, there may be no clear winner. But plenty of winners have chosen the 'Zook.

CHAPTER FIVE

THE WEE-STROM

Bigger isn't always better, and Suzuki proved it with the V-Strom 650 ABS. This bike still has a thirsty 645 cc (39 cubic inches) displacement, so it's not exactly a "little" engine that could, but it is littler than its big brother, the V-Strom 1000.

Suzuki used its popular SV650 bike as a blueprint for the engine, which offers a happy medium between performance and comfort. Enthusiasts have found the "Wee-Strom" to be comfortable but responsive, and versatile without feeling bland. In fact, when the first V-Strom 650 debuted in 2004, it rocketed to the top of the popularity charts, appealing to a wide range of riders. According to *Rider* magazine, "The V-Strom 650 developed a cult following and outsold its big brother by a healthy margin. It was the ideal do-it-all middleweight—peppy motor, rugged chassis, effortless handling, comfortable seating, 250-mile (402 km) range, and reasonable price. What's not to love?"

Suzuki has dubbed the V-Strom 650 "the comfortable adventure tourer," clearly identifying its dual goal for this midsize bike. Indeed, this bike is easy to manage without feeling flimsy, creating a smooth ride both on-road and off. Consumers also like its reasonable price tag and high fuel economy.

V is for versatile. Suzuki's V-Strom 650 offers a little bit of everything: power and performance, comfort and style. All that, combined with reliability, has helped it become one of Suzuki's most popular models.

The size of the engine puts this bike in the middleweight category, but numbers don't always tell the whole story. The additional cylinder in the V-twin engine makes the bike more powerful than others in its class, such as the Kawasaki KLR650, or BMW's 650GS Sertao. The rev limiter kicks in at 9,700 rpm, but casual (and even pretty demanding) riders will be happy with the 64 horsepower that the 650 delivers at 9,000 rpm. Torque is solid, too: the bike offers 42.7 lb-ft at 6,600 revs, and the numbers stay healthy all the way up to 8,000, when it finally eases up.

A finely tuned electronic fuel injection system allows the bike to start smoothly. Six gears—as opposed to the class average of five—in the transmission give the rider more control in the lower ranges, and allow a broad top gear for freeway cruising. Tweaks to the engine in the 2012 model also resulted in less drag from friction—enough so that Suzuki claimed fuel efficiency was boosted a remarkable 10 percent.

The Long Haul

As if the original model wasn't good enough, in the years after it debuted, Suzuki decided to upgrade the V-Strom 650 with several extras. One was an antilock brake system, offering improved traction and a safety net for tough riding conditions. The ABS works with in conjunction with two-piston calipers on the twin front discs, and a single disc on the rear. Suzuki also revamped the suspension, adjusting the support to better handle the inevitable bumps on the road.

WHAT'S IN A NAME?

Even the name of the V-Strom seems to confirm that it's a blend of power and personality. Suzuki put the "V" in the name to recognize the bike's V-twin engine. "Strom" comes from a German word that means "current." The 650 cc (40 cubic inches) version of the bike is nicknamed the "Wee-Strom" because it's smaller, or more "wee," than its 1,000 cc (61 cubic inches) big brother. The bike was first introduced in 2004, but newer models have seen some cosmetic changes, including two-tone paint and a smoother, more rounded look. One reviewer thought the new model looked like it belonged in a video game, prompting him to dub the bike the "Wii-Strom."

Settings were also adjusted to accommodate riders who want to test the limits of the bike's quick acceleration and braking but not get bucked off in the process. And hey—if you don't like it, it's easy to change. Suzuki made the whole thing very user-friendly: just rotate a dial to lock in the suspension settings that feel most comfortable.

The V-Strom comes equipped with a 61.4-inch (1,560 mm) wheelbase, and improved suspension that makes long rides comfortable. There are also hard-sided, locking saddlebags for packing lunch, tools, or a change of underwear. Add in an adjustable windscreen and seat height options that will accommodate riders who come on the short or tall side, and

Dedicated V-Strom riders might be tempted to leave the roadway and steer the Wee-Strom onto a gentle mountain trail for an extra dose of fun and adventure on an afternoon ride.

the V-Strom makes a comfortable ride overall. Other extras include heated grips and power outlets. On the downside, the high footpegs may cramp taller riders, and the 519-pound (235 kg) weight is heavier than its competitors and somewhat noticeable in corners.

Just because the bike is happy over a longer haul doesn't mean it can't rumble with the off-roaders if necessary. Suzuki classifies the V-Strom 650 as both an adventure bike and a dual-sport, meaning it can jump the curb and go to light trail riding. The V-strom excels more on the street side than the adventure side, however. This bike isn't built to take too much of a beating on pitted dirt roads or in heavy brush. The engine isn't socked away under a protective covering, so it could sustain damage in a spill. Among competitors in this class, the V-Strom faces challenges in the off-road portion but more than makes up for it in the touring aspect, making it a favorite among riders who really aren't doing that much hard-core trailing. And for those who want to double-up, the V-Strom makes it easy to take on a passenger.

The V-Strom's versatility has made it the bike of choice for some around-the-world travelers—think 40,000 miles (64,374 km) over eight months—and an editor at one motorcycle magazine liked it so much, she wouldn't give back the test model and bought it instead. A review in the *Telegraph* observes, "For the rider after a motorcycle as all-round transport without sacrificing the fun of two wheels, the V-Strom has proved thoroughly persuasive."

CHAPTER SIX

SETTING A STANDARD

not everyone has the build for a muscle bike, or the desire for the adrenaline rush delivered by an off-road excursion. But plenty of people have a little bit of an adventurous spirit. It's just enough to beckon them out of the confines of a car and onto the open road. For beginners, or for those who just want a little fun without the death-wish danger element, Suzuki offers the SFV650.

This standard bike started life in the late 1990s as the SV650, and it immediately became a hit in the middleweight market. *Rider* magazine reported on the splash it made: "When [the SV650] debuted in 1999, Suzuki's small-fry naked bike wowed the press and the public alike...Why? The SV650 had that special something not all bikes have. It can't be bolted on and it doesn't show up in spec charts. Character, soul, mojo, whatever you call it, the SV650 had it."

Ten years later, Suzuki updated the SV, giving it a descriptive name—the "Gladius." That's an old Latin word for a short, double-bladed sword used by Roman soldiers. The new name proved to be a good fit for the bike because the SFV650 delivered on two fronts: performance and reliability.

Behind the marketing language lurked basically the same engine, but that was a smart move on Suzuki's part. The 645 cc (39 cubic inches), liquid-cooled V-twin had proved endlessly reliable, without sacrificing performance. Sometimes, in the quest to tweak and improve, engineers are tempted to "fix what ain't broke," but in this case, they resisted the temptation and stuck with a good thing. The SFV650 is not a finicky or ornery machine. Ask it to start, and it does. Nor is it a show-off, with only a modest exhaust note. But just because it doesn't advertise, doesn't mean it can't deliver.

The SFV650 accelerates quickly and easily out of a stop, and it doesn't hiccup as it moves up through the revs, offering consistent power all the way to the 10,500 redline.

A splash of color just adds to the whimsical nature of the SFV650 Gladius, an everyday bike that looks at home anywhere it goes: city, highway—or even sitting in the driveway.

When the revs go into the middle and upper ranges—7,000 to 10,000—this bike has the muscle to deliver power that's stronger than the smooth ride would seem to indicate. It snorts out 71 horsepower at 8,400 rpm, and offers 42.9 lb-ft of torque at 7,400 revs. Meanwhile, it's got a broad power-band and smooth six-speed transmission that keep it reliable down around 4,000 rpm.

THE UJM

The SFV650 is a naked bike designed for everyday use. It's not overly weighted toward looks or supersport performance. In fact, it could be called a modern take on the classic universal Japanese motorcycle, or UJM. In the 1970s, *Cycle* magazine invented the term to describe standard motorcycles made by the "Big Four" Japanese manufacturers: Suzuki, Honda, Yamaha, and Kawasaki. Honda's CB750 was a classic example of the UJM, and it set the stage for later bikes, including Suzuki's GS750 and the Kawasaki Z1.

UJMs generally had four-cylinder, air-cooled, carbureted engines, and an upright seating position typical of standards. This versatile design made the bike a fit for riders with different styles and preferences and across a wide range of skill levels. *Cycle* magazine noted that the bikes were "conceived in sameness, executed with precision, and produced by the thousands." American riders snapped them up, and their popularity helped further the sport of motorcycling in the United States.

European Attitude

Styling has a definite European flair, with wide handlebars that provide a little bit of attitude, and sleek lines that flow from the headlight to the rear fender without a glitch. It's got all the style of an Italian bike and adds in Japanese efficiency in the engine. All in all, it's serious competition for other bikes in this class, such as the Ducati Monster 696 or Kawasaki's ER-6N. "[It comes with] an engine that's easier to live with on a daily basis than any of the Italian twin-cylinders, but one that's got heaps of attitude nonetheless," according to Moto123.com.

Steering is responsive, and the suspension ably handles almost any regular surface, although it gets a tad sketchy at higher speeds or on bumpy roads. Seating position is classic standard: upright enough to make a long-distance journey comfortable, but not so far reclined as to make navigating turns feel like they need to be done with a remote control. It's also accommodating for smaller riders. In fact, the SFV650 is a perfect commuter bike. It nicely negotiates the ins and outs of traffic, offering competent cornering, but without the uncomfortable crouch that won't work on a longer ride. There is, however, a short ground clearance, so scraping is a hazard during tight turns.

The steel chassis adds some weight, and at 446 pounds (202 kg), the SFV650 tips the scales more than others in its class. However, the balanced frame makes it easier to handle than the overall weight would suggest, while a 56.9-inch (1,445 mm) wheelbase keeps it stable

It's easy to put the SFV650 through its paces on the open road, but this cooperative bike is also a breeze to navigate through traffic. A standard seating position helps with comfort on longer rides.

but not a stick-in-the-mud. Dual-piston calipers on the twin disc brakes on the front, and a single on the rear, bring things to a stop. For the environmentally minded, an improved exhaust system cuts down on overall emissions.

Most motorcyclists aren't going to take four-month world tours or dig through the wild and woolly underbrush on two wheels. Instead, they ride a few miles at a time, through traffic rather than tumbleweeds. The SFV650 offers the blend of practicality and performance that make those trips fun.

SPECIFICATION CHART

HAYABUSA

Redline	11,000 rpm
Horsepower	171 hp at 9,800 rpm
Torque	101.7 ft-lb at 7,300 rpm
Transmission	6-speed
Fuel capacity	5.5 gallons / 20.9 liters

BOULEVARD M109R

Redline	7,500 rpm
Horsepower	127 at 6,200 rpm
Torque	117 lb-ft at 3,200 rpm
Transmission	5-speed
Fuel capacity	5.2 gallons / 19.7 liters

GSX-R1000

Redline	13,300
Horsepower	168 hp at 11,800 rpm
Torque	79.2 lb-ft at 10,400 rpm
Transmission	6-speed
Fuel capacity	4.6 gallons / 17.4 liters

RM-Z450

Redline	11,000
Horsepower	51.9 at 8,900
Torque	33.2 lb-ft at 7,600
Transmission	5-speed
Fuel capacity	1.6 gallons / 6.1 liters

V-STROM 650

Redline	9,700 rpm
Horsepower	64.4 at 9,000 rpm
Torque	42.7 lb-ft at 6,600 rpm
Transmission	6-speed
Fuel capacity	5.3 gallons / 20.1 liters

SFV650

Redline	10,500 rpm
Horsepower	67.1 hp at 9,000 rpm
Torque	42.9 lb-ft at 7,400 rpm
Transmission	6-speed
Fuel capacity	3.8 gallons / 14.4 liters

GLOSSARY

ALLOY A metal made from two or more different metals.

DAMPING The process of controlling how much suspension is delivered.

DRIVE MODE A setting that controls how power is delivered.

ERGONOMICS Materials and designs used to improve physical comfort.

EXHAUST NOTE The distinctive sound a motorcycle makes.

FAIRING A covering on the front portion of a motorcycle offering wind protection.

FORK Metal tubes that connect the front wheel to the motorcycle frame.

MOTOCROSS A type of motorcycle race held on closed, rough circuits.

NAKED BIKE A bike with little or no fairings or additional bodywork.

POWERBAND The range of revolutions per minute (rpm) in which a bike performs most effectively.

REDLINE The highest limit of the engine's revolutions per minute (rpm).

SUPERBIKE A sport bike with a displacement of 1,000 cc (61 cubic inches) or more.

TORQUE The tendency of a force to produce a rotation.

FOR MORE INFORMATION

American Motorcyclist Association (AMA)
13515 Yarmouth Drive
Pickerington, OH 43147
(800) 262-5646
Web site: http://www.americanmotorcyclist.com
Founded in 1924, the AMA is the world's largest motorcycling
organization. It works to promote the motorcycling lifestyle
and protect the interests of riders.

American Suzuki
P.O. Box 1100
Brea, CA 92822
(714) 572-1490
Web site: www.suzukicycles.com
Suzuki's American headquarters has information on the compa-
ny's product line and provides assistance to Suzuki customers.

Motorcycle Safety Foundation (MSF)
2 Jenner, Suite 150
Irvine, CA 92618
(800) 446-9227
Web site: http://online2.msf-usa.org
Sponsored by several major motorcycle manufactures, the MSF
offers courses in safe, responsible motorcycle operation and
advocates for safer riding conditions for motorcyclists.

Motorcycle Sport Touring Association (MSTA)
P.O. Box 2187

Manchaca, TX 78652
Web site: http://www.ridemsta.com
The MSTA organizes events for sport touring motorcylists
  and unites enthusiasts of this branch of motorcycling.

National Motorsport Association (NMA)
P.O. Box 891299
Temecula, CA 92589
(951) 587-9805
Web site: http://www.nmamx.com
The NMA, founded in 1970, sponsors the World Mini Grand
  Prix, an annual motocross competition for young riders.

Suzuki Owners Club USA
P.O. Box 338
Cheltenham, MD 20623-0338
Web site: http://www.soc-usa.org
The Suzuki Owners Club USA is a sister organization to the
  main branch located in the United Kingdom. It provides a
  social framework for riders of Suzuki motorcycles.

Web Sites

Due to the changing nature of Internet links, Rosen Publishing has developed an online list of Web sites related to the
subject of this book. This site is updated regularly. Please use
this link to access the list:

http://www.rosenlinks.com/MOTO/Suzu

FOR FURTHER READING

Adamson, Thomas K. *Motocross Racing* (Blazers: Dirt Bike World). North Mankato, MN: Capstone Press, 2010.

Ames, Michael, and Jonny Fuego. *Cruisers*. Layton, UT: Gibbs Smith, 2009

David, Jack. *Enduro Motorcycles.* Minneapolis, MN: Bellwether Media, 2008.

Doeden, Matt. *Enduro Racing* (Blazers: Dirt Bike World). North Mankato, MN: Capstone Press, 2010.

Gillespie, Lisa Jane. *Motorcycles*. London, England: Usborne Books, 2011.

Henshaw, Peter. *The Encyclopedia of Motorcycles, Vol. 5: Suzuki-ZZR.* New York, NY: Chelsea House Publishers, 2000.

Holter, James. *Dirt Bike Racers* (Kid Racers). Berkeley Heights, NJ: Enslow Publishers, 2010.

Mason, Paul. *Dirt Biking: The World's Most Remarkable Dirt Bike Rides and Techniques.* North Mankato, MN: Capstone Press, 2011.

Oxlade, Chris. *Motorcycles* (How Things Work). Collingwood, Ontario, Canada: Saunders Book Company, 2011.

Stealey, Bryan. *Motocross* (Racing Mania). Tarrytown, NY: Marshall Cavendish, 2009.

Streissguth, Thomas. *Standard Motorcycles*. Minneapolis, MN: Bellwether Media, 2008

West, Phil. *Superbikes: Machines of Dreams* (Gearhead Mania). New York, NY: Rosen Classroom, 2012.

Young, Jeff. *Motorcycles: The Ins and Outs of Superbikes, Choppers, and Other Motorcycles.* North Mankato, MN: Capstone Press, 2010.

BIBLIOGRAPHY

Ash, Kevin. "Suzuki GSX-R1000 Review." *Telegraph*, March 4, 2012. Retrieved December 28, 2012 (http://www.telegraph .co.uk/motoring/motorbikes/9108554/Suzuki-GSX-R1000 -review.html).

Bastien, Pascal. "2012 Suzuki SFV 650 Gladius Review." Moto123.com, November 4, 2012. Retrieved December 22, 2012 (http://www.moto123.com/motorcycle-reviews/ article,2012-suzuki-sfv-650-gladius-review.spy?artid=149351).

Dawes, Justin. "2011 Suzuki Boulevard M109R Comparison." *Motorcycle USA*, June 20, 2011. Retrieved December 28, 2012 (http://www.motorcycle-usa.com/238/10325/Motorcycle -Article/2011-Suzuki-Boulevard-M109R-Comparison.aspx).

Denison, Chris. "2013 Suzuki RM-Z450—First Impression." Dirt *Rider*, August 2, 2012. Retrieved December 18, 2012 (http:// www.dirtrider.com/tests/2013-suzuki-rm-z450-first-impression).

Waheed, Adam. "2012 Suzuki GSX-1300R Hayabusa Comparison." *Motorcycle USA*, April 30, 2012. Retrieved December 22,2012 (http://www.motorcycle-usa.com/232/12923/ Motorcycle-Article/2012-Suzuki-GSX-1300R-Hayabusa -Comparison.aspx).

Williams, Don. "2012 Suzuki V-Strom 650 Adventure." *Ultimate Motorcycling*, July 10, 2012. Retrieved December 18, 2012 (http://ultimatemotorcycling.com/2012-suzuki-v-strom-650 -adventure-review).

INDEX

About the Author

Diane Bailey has written more than thirty nonfiction books for teens, on subjects ranging from sports to states to celebrities. She has two sons and two dogs and lives in Kansas.

Photo Credits

Designer: Brian Garvey; Editor Bethany Brian; Photo Researcher; Amy Feinberg